Not for Rent,
Sale, or Lease

Angela,
May only good Things
befall You!.
Velma DuPont

Not for Rent, Sale, or Lease

Poetic Illuminations from a Woman's Heart

Velma Miller DuPont

To order additional copies of this book, contact:
Xlibris Corporation
1-888-795-4274
www.Xlibris.com
Orders@Xlibris.com
41412

CONTENTS

Acknowledgments 11

SUITE 1: CHURCH HUMOR

Sistah So-and-So 17
Let the Church Roll On 19
Salvation Is Free, But I Ain't 22
Sunday Dinner 23

SUITE 2: ENTHRALLMENT

Finally 29
Day After Day 30
Fantasy Lover 31
Your Arms Speak to Me 32
A Man's Got to Move Me 33
I Always Knew There Was More 34
Stay 35
Thirst Quencher 36
Good-bye 37

SUITE 3: A MYRIAD OF EXPRESSIONS

Not For Rent, Sale, or Lease 41
Fire 42
My Life 43
Wake Up! 44
Numb 45
Shut Up and Listen! 46
Legacy 47
Where's Your Joy? 48

A Willing Sacrifice 49

First Class, Second Class, No Class at All 50

Imprints 52

Mark My Words 53

Let Me Ride, Daddy 54

Nobody Knows 56

Scared No More 58

The 4 *M*'s 59

I Heard What You *Didn't* Say 60

My Old Iron 61

Broke 62

Why? 63

Layaway Love 64

It's Over Now 65

Need Is a Four-letter Word 66

You Don't Deserve My Love 67

Happily Single 68

Ladies, Listen Up! 69

Separating the Men From the Boys 70

Men 72

SUITE 4: ENCOURAGEMENT AND INSPIRATION

Perfect Peace 75

He Understands 77

He Comforts 78

Look to the Cross 79

From Morning till Night 80

He Is Our Hope 81

You Better Come Clean With God 82

Where You Gonna Sit When You Git to Hebben? 83

A Prayer 84

Mamee 85

The Family 86

The Gift of Giving 87

Miss Magnolia 88

Much Harvesting 89

Rhythms of Life 90

Music 91

Free.. 92
Happiness 93
Celebrate Life!.. 94
Do You Know Where You're Going? 95
Don't Give In! Don't Give Out! Don't Give Up!............................... 96
Destiny 97
Just Keep On! 98
The Triumph Of Light 99
Don't Worry 'bout the Mule; You Just Load the Wagon 100

To my mother, Mrs. Carrie Mae Miller (Mamee)

A million volumes could be filled with my love for you, Mamee, for much of what I am, and ever shall be, is purely because of thee.

ACKNOWLEDGMENTS

My Heavenly Father,
from whom all blessings flow, I thank you for the loan
of such wondrous and divine gifts.

Thankfulness is lifted up to my ancestors—may their spirit
of courage, faith, and might abide in me and in their posterity
till kingdom come.

Grateful acknowledgment is also made to my ten siblings
(Lenus [Billy], George, Larry, Eddie [Skip], Aaron
Sabrina, Warren, Gary, Garland, and Genesis),
who unwittingly served as subjects of inspiration
for some of these writings.
Thanks for making room for me in the litter.

Bill, my steadfast friend, I thank you for your unwavering belief
in me and your enthusiastic support for all my endeavors.

Roro, thank you for your friendship and
your generous consultative and technical support.

To you, Flash Aytanm—thank you for illuminating my life.

And last, I extend my deepest gratitude
to the one who sat behind me, the few who sat beside me,
the many who sat in the back of my mind,
and the incalculable unnamed who contributed
in untold ways to the fruition and success of this book.

My friends, I give you

NOT FOR RENT, SALE, OR LEASE
Poetic Illuminations from a Woman's Heart

May the words within
delight, enthrall, enlighten, provoke,
and inspire your being.

VELMA MILLER DUPONT

SUITE 1

CHURCH HUMOR

SISTAH SO-AND-SO

(That Sistah So-and-So is somethin' else!)

Shhhhhhh!

Here comes Sistah So-and-So
Struttin' down the aisle
Pushin' past the ushers
Showin' off her style.

Church started over an hour ago
Yet she's just gittin' in
She comes this late on ev'ry Sunday
I tell ya, child, it's a sin.

She can't ever git here on time
'Cause with herself, she's makin' a fuss
But she gonna have to quit makin' an entrance
And come early like the rest of us.

'Cause ev'ry Sunday, the doors swing open
And she stands there lookin' proud
The preacher stops preachin'; the choir stops singin'
And Brother Deacon utters out loud.

"Lawd, have mercy on my soul"
But to the Lawd, he ain't talkin'
Nooo! Both of his eyes are completely glued
To Sistah So-and-So as she's walkin'.

Just look at her struttin' and swishin' down the aisle
Her dress is hoist up all yonder
Exposin' ever'thang she's got
Don't leave no room to wonder.

And she knows exactly what she's doin'
Oh! She knows it very well
But you see, she already done reserved
Her one-way ticket to hell.

'Cause she don't come to worship the Lawd
And she don't come to praise
Nooo! She just come to stir up trouble
And cause the brothers to gaze.

And gaze they do, all up and down
Lawd knows what they thinkin' is fright'nin'
But one of these days, while they lookin'
They all gonna be struck by lightnin'.

But she do look good, I have to admit
'Cause around her, the brothers do prance
But I just wish she'd stop some of that primpin'
And give the rest of us sisters a chance!

LET THE CHURCH ROLL ON

It's Sunday morning, the church bells chime
    Sunday school won't start on time
Church filling up, just like it's Easter Day
    Some come to look, and some come to pray
Some come to sing, and some come to shout
    But some come to hear what the Word's about
Menfolk I've never seen, looking so fine
    Pants all creased and shoes spit-shined
Children resplendent in their Sunday best
    Mama's looking good in her layaway dress
Hair hot combed and relaxed bone-straight
    If I don't get moving, I'm gonna be late
The saints are doing the Sunday morning meet and greet
    Nobody better be sitting in my seat
Sisters grinning teeth and batting their eyes
    Short skirts exposing forbidden thighs
Missionaries in front of me with wide-brimmed hats
    Don't they know I can't see over that
Fast Fannie comes late, trying to get folks' attention
    Oh! There's one more thing I forgot to mention
The deacons have called a top secret meeting
    Trying to find out which one of them is cheating
Look at that deaconess, so pious and smug
    Climbing down from her pedestal to give me a fake hug
The evangelist's face looks so stern and holy
    Feet doing the dance called the holy-roly
Choir director signals—she's ready to sing *her* song
    Inspirational devotion is taking too long

Organ, drums, and tambourines
    The choir marches in with the same old routine
When the pastor makes his entrance, everybody must rise
    Congregation is straining to catch his eyes
Preacher grunts and starts doing his holy prance
    All the single sisters are so entranced
He delivers a sermon that's all improvised
    Preaches for two hours, to no one's surprise
Preaching about sin and folks backsliding
    Convicting folks so hard that they come out of hiding
Preacher pleads the blood on the saints and the sinners
    And even on Brother Cecil, the lottery winner
Ushers with collection plates, following the drill
    Going back for change for a dollar bill
The baptism water is chilly and cold
    Just waiting to purify a sin-sick soul
Congregation praising with uplifted hands
    Funeral home fans choreograph a breezy dance
Folks on bended knees, witnessing for the Lord
    The morning train's coming; I hope they get on board
The clerk goes to the altar, she's so distraught
    Nobody knows what she did, but she must've gotten caught
Trustees in the corner, issuing out blame
    Be careful, or they might scandalize *your* name
Sistah So-and-So is about to have another wedding
    She better hurry up because the rumors are spreading

The bride is getting married, all dressed in white
    On her fifth marriage; now, you know that's not right
Folks gossiping about the deacons and the preacher too
    And, sister, they will surely talk about you
Sunday school children learn about Peter and Paul
    Downstairs, they're running and playing in the fellowship hall
Stewards arguing over money for the church's reunion
    Children sneaking to steal leftover communion
Cooks in the kitchen, fussing over their cakes
    Everybody wants to fix the pastor's plate
The members start lining up for the collation
    That cup down there is for your donation
Hospitality club selling fish and chicken plates
    There'll be plenty of them left even if you get there late
Auxiliaries raising money for the building fund
    How much in the treasury? I heard there's none
Quarterly church meetings, all out of control
    Folks going to hell and losing their soul
Church folks need to stop all their mess
    And fall down on their knees and confess
If they don't stop the madness, the church is doomed
    Don't y'all know He's coming soon?
And if church folks just can't seem to get along
    Let's vote to sweep 'em out, and let the church roll on!

SALVATION IS FREE, BUT I AIN'T

Hey!

Did I tell you about that jackleg preacher
That I went out with the other night
And when it came time to pay for the dinner
How he put up an awful fight?

He refused to pay for our dinner
He said the food wasn't worth that much
Then, he started mumbling to me about money
While counting nickels and pennies and such.

Now, he knew he didn't have any money
Yet had the gall to ask me out to dine
But when he asked me to pay for the dinner
I said, "Reverend, you must be out of your mind!"

But I should have known he didn't have any money
Because all through dinner, he preached to me
About the world and the high cost of living
And how he was so glad salvation is free.

Now, I'm a church-going lady, but I was getting upset
And I didn't know whether to sit there or flee
So I broke it on down where he could understand
And, child, I almost lost my dignity.

"I have had enough of your preaching
Your behavior ain't fittin' for the ministry"
But he still said that he won't pay for nothing
As long as salvation is free.

Embarrassed, I made that slickster take me home
I lied, said I was feeling kind of faint
And when he asked me if he could kiss me good night
I said, "Salvation is free, but I ain't!"

SUNDAY DINNER

1. *(That fried chicken is calling my name.)*

My momma's in the kitchen with Aunt Mable
She's tryin' to get Sunday dinner on the table
The chicken is fryin'
Hungry children are cryin'
And she's doin' the very best that she's able.

Deacon Sherman is droppin' by for dinner today
Said our house just happened to be on his way
But I just can't determine
How it is that Deacon Sherman
Only drops by on the Lord's day.

Now, he knows Momma's a very good cook
And he sho' 'nuff likes the way that she looks
But if he thinks Momma's inclined
Well then, he's out of his mind
But he's tryin' to get Momma by hook or by crook.

For Momma's chicken, everybody comes down
And one chicken ain't enough to go around
So in order to be served
You've got to reserve
Yo' piece while it can still be found.

Around the stove, are the nappy-headed chaps
They don't know it, but they 'bout to get slapped
'Cause once that chicken leaves the skillet
Yo' piece, they just might steal it
And all that's left for you will be the scraps.

Momma takes her seasonings down from the rack
She flours the chicken in a brown paper sack
In first go thighs and breasts
And then go all the rest
Yeah! Liver, gizzard, neck, and the back.

Momma's chicken is the best I've ever had
And one piece is just enough to make me mad
Once you taste that golden crust
Then, your mouth might wanna cuss
And if you miss yo' piece, then that's just too bad.

My mouth waters for Momma's macaroni and cheese
And I smell the okra with the black-eyed peas
And Momma's tangy potato salad
Will surely seduce my palate
'Cause those are Momma's spe-ci-al-i-ties.

Uncle Ben is cooling off up on the shelf
Every grain is sittin' off by itself
That rice is fluffy and white
And steamed just right
Why, there won't be any of that left.

Momma's sweet potato pie has honey and spice
And her love is mixed up in it, to be precise
Cinnamon and nutmeg are swirlin'
Creamy butter is twirlin'
Now, you know I'm gonna git me a slice.

When we see Momma turn the fire down
We know the chicken is fried up crisp and golden brown
Then that special moment comes
Onions mingle with the crumbs
And that brown gravy floatin' all around.

But first, Momma says that we must ask the blessin'
And we know just who Momma is addressin'
Deacon Sherman clears his throat
And then, he 'cites a Bible quote
But now, it's Momma's chicken that he's assessin'.

"Everybody, close your eyes and bow your heads
And let us all heed the words that Jesus said
'Man don't live by bread alone'
I would like 'de wishbone
Pass the collard greens and the corn bread."

2. (After Sunday dinner)

With guts full, we retired to the den
And Deacon Sherman started to harp about sin
But when he started praying
We didn't care what he was saying
We just nodded our heads and said, "Amen."

He leaned back in the recliner for a nap
Surrounded by all those nappy-headed chaps
Although Deacon is good-hearted
He sat right there and farted
And it was time for us to call that show a wrap.

It was impossible to get him to leave
He said he'd come back next Sunday eve
Then he asked for aluminum foil
And that made my momma recoil
And now *that*, I could hardly believe.

But wait! He asked my momma out for a date
And at the same time, he asked her for a plate
Momma lost her religion
Didn't give him a smidgen
And said, "Pick me up at the pearly gates."

Dinner is over, and we've eaten all we can
Momma starts to put away her fryin' pan
Momma's family is fulfilled
With such a stupendous meal
And next Sunday, Momma will do it all again!

3. (There's more.)

About that deacon? Momma had to take a stand
Because her Sunday dinners were suddenly in demand
But no more *deacons* came for dinner
After she invited Reverend Skinner
Praise the Lord! One meal, and he asked for Momma's hand!

Amen.

SUITE 2

ENTHRALLMENT

FINALLY

I've been loved the way
I always dreamed I'd be loved
Took him long enough
But he finally arrived
Our season, we couldn't deny.

I want nothing else
To him, no one could measure
I am now fulfilled
He lingered long at my door
After him, there'll be no more.

DAY AFTER DAY

(Inspired by CDW)

Day after day
I sit watching you
And night after night
My dreams are of you
But when the morning comes
And daylight appears
I must shake myself
And wipe away the tears
Because day after day
Day after day
Night after night
I dream of you.

It's funny
Sometimes I wonder if you care
Oh! Somehow you must
Remember the moments that we shared
And, darling, since that time
You've been on my mind
I beg you to tell me
What I must do
Because day after day
Day after day
Night after night
I dream of you.

Because day after day, night after night
I dream of you.

FANTASY LOVER

I finally found the perfect man
But it's not what it seems
He's only perfect for one reason
He exists only in my dreams
Because in my dreams
He's whatever I want him to be
There's no pain, and there's no misery
There's nothing but love
And he treats me like no other
He's my fantasy lover.

My perfect man is always loving
He's tender, sweet, and never mean
He's all I've ever hoped and prayed for
Yet he exists only in my dreams
Because in my dreams
He's whatever I want him to be
There's no pain, and there's no misery
There's nothing but love
And he treats me like no other
He's my fantasy lover.

Sometimes I wish this man was real
But then, I remember what I've seen
And when I view reality
I'm glad that he lives in my dreams
Because in my dreams
He's whatever I want him to be
There's no pain, and there's no misery
There's nothing but love
And he treats me like no other
He's my fantasy lover.

YOUR ARMS SPEAK TO ME

Your arms speak to me.
They whisper,
>   "I'll be your strength and protector
>   Lean wholly upon me
>   Shield yourself beneath me
>   In me, find refuge."

Your arms speak to me.
They declare,
>   "I am your gateway
>   Enter, and I will lead you to sweet serenity
>   I will caress you as thunder is caressed in a rampaging storm
>   In me, find comfort and solace."

Your arms speak to me.
They implore,
>   "Let me blanket you with my love
>   Let me suffocate you with tantalizing warmth
>   Let me saturate you with seductive calm
>   In me, find hidden compassion."

Your arms speak to me.
They shout,
>   "Come! Within me, you will be engulfed so fully,
>   so wonderfully, so magically, that your only
>   utterance will be your groaning, beckoning, and
>   imploring scream for me to speak louder!"

Umm!
Your arms speak to me!
And I perceive every word!

A MAN'S GOT TO MOVE ME

How does a man move me?

Intellectual intercourse
Sings me a song
Writes me a sonnet
Plays with me and prays with me
Teases me and pleases me
Dances with me
Wrestles with me
Whispers sweet *and* naughty ditties in my ears
Possesses suavity, sensuousness, dexterity
He makes an eruption of Mount St. Helens seem like a hiccup. Uh!

Laughter, much laughter
Excitement
Brilliance escorts him into every room
Lives life over the speed limit
Selfless and sacrificing
Offers his last dime to a hungry vagabond
Gives me a Valentine ragweed bouquet he picked from my backyard
Always wanting to do something for me—can fix stuff too
Drives 100 miles to wake me so we can watch the sunrise together
He cooks, serves me, washes the dishes, *and* takes out the trash.

Patience
Listens endlessly—he lets me talk all day and cry all night
Dries my scalding, salty tears with his luscious lips
Devoted enough to console me when I am sick and exasperated
Juvenescent enough to give me a horsy ride anytime I want one
Lets me yap all through the playoff games; never once says "shuddy"
Bold, confident, and unafraid to tell me when to "cut"
Sensitive enough to say he's sorry, strong enough to say he's wrong
Humble enough to ask for help without feeling emasculated
He proclaims he would surrender his life for me.

How does a man move me?
That's how a man moves me.

I ALWAYS KNEW THERE WAS MORE

I always knew there was more.

You stretched a ladder to the moon
        and plucked a star from its midst for me

You methodically reconfigured the elements of the firmament
        for my earthly bliss

You procured the infinite and superfluous gains of the universe,
        and you nestled them at my feet

You unbarred, unlatched, and unchained
        your vaulted, imprisoned heart so I could enter

You renounced all that was dear to you
        so that you might forever prove your eternal love for me

And for all my other desires, you summoned and commissioned
        a phalanx of angels and mortals to serve me

I always knew there was more; now, I have it all.

STAY

(For CJ, "B. Most High")

You came into my life
You walked right in, and you sat down
And now that you are in
It seems I always want you around.

Darling, you slid into my heart
And I didn't even know you were there
But now that you are here
It sometimes seems more than I can bear
Because from the second that you touched me
To the minute that you cared
And from the hours that we lay there
Through the mornings that we shared
You were there.

Darling, you came into my life
And in my life, I hope you will stay.

THIRST QUENCHER

So you say you're thirsty
But water won't do
Well, how about I pour myself
Into a cup for you

But once you raise the cup of me . . .

GOOD-BYE

Don't leave without me
I shan't draw another breath
I dare not go on.

We only subsist
When our hearts are intertwined
If you cease, I cease.

If your curtain draws
As you climb the crystal stair
I'll be close behind.

SUITE 3

A MYRIAD OF EXPRESSIONS

NOT FOR RENT, SALE, OR LEASE

Don't think you can buy me with your trinkets
Or your sweet, melodious words
For there's nothing you can say to me
I haven't already heard.

And don't think you can entice me with romancing
And those fancy, indulgent feasts
For you must remember, darling
I'm not for rent, sale, or lease.

And please don't be mistaken, for I am not impressed
With your position, power, or pedigree
You see, I'm less impressed with transitory things
But more with character, honor, and integrity.

So for all the things you proffer
Humph! Your motives—you might as well cease
For I must remind you, darling
I'm not for rent, sale, or lease.

But oh! A price does rest upon my head
And when it's met, I'm yours for the asking
It is when to the table is brought
A dual level of commitment and love everlasting.

It's when in all things, we soar together
And we discover life's elusive peace
And then, you'll know for certain, darling
That I'm not for rent, sale, or lease!

FIRE

You can't put **1** log on the fire and expect to stay warm all winter!

MY LIFE

My life didn't begin with you
My life won't end with you
Therefore, **My** existence is not dependent upon you.

WAKE UP!

Wake up!

Shake yourself from your slippery, slumbering stupor
Detach yourself from your dusty, dingy dungeon
Crawl out from your chilly, confined closet
Climb out of your suffocating cocoon
And get in the crosshairs of life!

Go ahead!
I dare you to justify your existence!
Wake up!
Get up!
Move!
Live!
Don't sleep so much!
You will have plenty of time to sleep when you're dead!

NUMB

Turn it off
Turn off the television
I can't look at the news
I leave the room to escape the barrage of noise
The onslaught follows me to the bathroom
I can still hear it.

Turn it off
Turn off the radio
I can't listen to the news
Cabbie, please turn it off
Let me ride in peace
And not be bombarded with the invasion of these fools.

These crazy, conniving, calamitous fools
Kill one another over the nothingness
That is forever tattooed on their lives
These crazy fools
Massacre their kindred one by one
Until whole generations are annihilated.

Searing crimson blood flows in the streets and drains in the gutters
Forever dyeing the grass with the innards of our youth
Forever suffocating the little saplings
Straining to emerge through hot city asphalt
Our attics will flood with the tears of mothers
Whose hearts refuse to continue beating while their offspring die.

Turn it off
Turn off the news
I can't bear to hear any more
It's not that I don't care
I care
But now, I am numb.

SHUT UP AND LISTEN!

If you just Shut Up and Listen, the universe will speak to you,
and the multiplicity of its being will become yours.

LEGACY

Start paying off your debt
I know you've heard this all before
Those before you sacrificed much
That you might rightfully walk through life's door
Now that you have an exalted, identifiable station in life
Now that your destination is clear
You can live and thrive as a man and not as a boy
You can realize your purpose and have nothing to fear
You have a revered legacy to uphold
As the beneficiary of gifts gained by sacrificial bones
You are indebted to posterity
And you are to ensure the legacy is forever known
May the legacy be manifest, and may we never forget
Shoulder your responsibility, and start paying off your debt.

WHERE'S YOUR JOY?

You say you've got joy in your heart?
Well, I don't believe it! Why not?
> You walk around with your face all twisted up as if you are mad God
> even bothered to wake you up this morning.

You say you've got joy in your soul?
Well, I don't believe it! Why not?
> Every word that comes out of your mouth is negative and
> there's something wrong with everybody, except you.

You say you've got Jesus and that's enough?
Well, I don't believe it! Why not?
> You're always complaining about what you don't have
> and you act as if the world owes you something.

You say the devil is a liar?
Well, I don't believe it! Why not?
> You go to every retreat, prayer meeting, and Bible study you
> can find, yet you are downtrodden, and you reek of misery.

That's right! I don't believe any of your holy pronouncements!
Because if you've got joy in your heart, as you proclaim
If you've got joy in your soul, as you proclaim
  If you've got Jesus in your life, as you proclaim
    If the devil is a liar, as you proclaim
      Then joy ought to radiate from your face
        Joy ought to shout in your utterances
          Joy ought to dance in your feet
            And joy ought to be emblazoned all over your life!

Where is your joy?

A WILLING SACRIFICE

Would you suffer through famine to fill another's cup
Your very last morsel—do you think you'd give it up?

Would you give of yourself and your precious little time
What about your money—would you give your last dime?

Would you give a little extra, not just what you could afford?
Would you make a willing sacrifice, if for you, there's no reward?

What sacrifice are you willing to make?

FIRST CLASS, SECOND CLASS, NO CLASS AT ALL

Born in a lineage of blue-blood pedigree
      Or everybody is wondering *whose could it be?*
Raised in a mansion that's high on a hill
      Or in a one-room shack behind the paper mill
Exclusive estate on a prime cul-de-sac
      Or a double-wide trailer by the railroad tracks
Dignified, refined, and of a superior class
      Or drink your Kool-Aid from a jelly glass
Esteemed credentials and a college degree
      Or an earned-at-night-school GED
Position, power, and worldly fame
      Or nobody ever remembers your name
Doctor, lawyer, and exalted brigadier
      Or waitress, cook, and maintenance engineer
Fair-haired brood with the finest means
      Or a meager diet of pinto beans
Money in the bank and money to throw away
      Or dodge the bill collector until the next payday
Rolls Royce, Jaguar, and Mercedes Benz
      Or trudge to get your groceries on bus no. 10
Holidays in Europe and Montreal
      Or Friday night hanging out at Buddy's Pool Hall
Chartered limousines and executive class
      Or get to where you're going by walking fast
Beluga caviar and the finest champagne
      Or eat your pork 'n' beans and don't complain
Afternoon tea at the fabulous Ritz
      Or fry up a breakfast of fish and grits
Tennis, polo, and a match of cricket
      Or run to the corner store to buy your lottery ticket
Furs, diamonds, and trinkets galore
      Or a cute little jewelry set from the dollar store
High-fashion designer clothes, dressed to kill
      Or used clothes bought down at the Goodwill
All the wondrous things that life demands
      Or wait till the "by-and-by" when you'll understand

Don't get caught up in the class-division game
And don't covet the things of others
> because you don't know what price they had to pay to attain it
>> or what price they have to pay to sustain it.

Don't allow anyone else to determine your worth
You are already important—because of Him
> And whatever your station in life, it's *your* station
>> and if it's all right with you, then it's all right; if not, *alter it.*

But first, find YOU; then, be YOU
BE the best YOU.

Whatever you are
Whatever you do
Whatever you have
JUST BE YOU!

Think about this:
If we're all on an airplane and that airplane goes
down
>down
>>down

Everybody goes down . . . first class, second class, no class at all.

> ***There are two times in life when class won't matter to you:***
> ***when you're born, and when you die.***

IMPRINTS

When you go someplace, let folks know you've been there.

MARK MY WORDS

("Thanks for nothing, Grandma.")

Grandma was always scoffing at the boy
"You ain't *nothing* now, and you never will be *nothing*"
And he would hang his little head and sigh
And because he believed
Grandma's words were really true
There was no need for him to try.

    And try, he didn't
    For he believed his life was doomed
    And Grandma's promise soon would ring true
    His days melted into months
    And the months into years
    And he did *nothing*, for *nothing* was all that he knew.

And for countless years after
Grandma's warning he would carry
Her prophetic words rang loudly in his ears
And when opportunities knocked
No courage had he, as a man
For his self-doubt had given way to fear.

    And his fear and his anger
    Would soon catapult him
    Into a cesspit of destruction and despair
    And land him in jail
    For the rest of his life
    All because he believed no one cared.

And the nothingness and fear
Consumed the boy and the man
Devoured and swallowed them up, so I've heard
And now, boy and man are gone
But oh! It's really *nothing*
Oh! The power of Grandma's words!

Watch what you say,
and never underestimate the recollection of a child.

LET ME RIDE, DADDY

Strolling down Clay Street on a Sunday afternoon
The sun is blistering
Walking hand in hand with my daddy
Daddy and his Raggedy Ann—"Raggedy Ann" is my nickname
Still got on my Sunday clothes
Still got on my gold patent leather Mary Janes too
I was in such a hurry to go jaunting with my daddy
I didn't even change into my play clothes after church
This was the first time Mama had ever agreed
To let me wear my Sunday clothes
To go walking with my daddy
But I don't want to walk with Daddy, I want to ride!

  "Bend over, Daddy! Bend over and let me ride!"

Daddy squats down real low and bends over
I climb up on his back and wrap my skinny arms around his neck
Daddy clamps his elbows around my legs good and tight
He stamps his pigeon-toed feet on the sidewalk, and we're off
Daddy likes to act like a real horse when we play "horsy"
Daddy is soooo funny.

  "Okay, Daddy! Now giddyup! Giddyup, horsy, giddyup!"

Whee! I'm riding horsy with my daddy
Daddy goes galloping up Clay Street like a "bat outta hell"
The wind is pulling my thick, greasy plaits back
The afterchurch sun is scorching my face
My panties are bunching up in my tail
But I just hold on tight to Daddy
And Daddy holds on tight to me
I lean my face against Daddy's back
I can smell the Prince Albert loose tobacco in his whiskers
And there's a faint hint of that musk aftershave he likes so much
Boy! Daddy's sweat, fused with those scents, just hypnotizes me
I love riding horsy with my daddy!

Daddy is loping so hard that my little hind part is sore
And my starched, perfectly ironed dress is now drenched with sweat
I'm starting to get tired, and I'm really starting to get sleepy
Just bobbing up and down on Daddy's back
I start to slide off Daddy's back, but I know he won't let me fall
Daddy's running and snorting just like a real racehorse
He looks and sounds so funny, I giggle out loud
We've been gone for over an hour; he says we'll have to stop soon
He looks back at me, grins, and gives a really loud yelp
Then, he bucks up for one more gallop
Finally, we slow our gait and start to trot on home
I'm exhausted, but I'm not satisfied—I want to ride some more.

"Just one more ride, Daddy! Just one more, please!"

"Baby, that's enough for today.
You know your daddy's got plenty horsy rides for
you. We'll go again next Sunday. Okay, Rags?"

"Okay, Daddy."

I'm just grinning, I'm just grinning
I can't wait for my next horsy ride with my daddy
I am so lucky
Every baby girl should be so lucky to ride horsy with her daddy
I lovvvvvvve riding horsy with Daddy!

HEY! SNAP OUT OF IT!
I wish I had been that lucky
It would have been great if that had ever happened, right?

It's just me, daydreaming again and wishing for a horsy ride with Daddy,
a horsy ride that never happened and never will happen, except in my
imagination. How sad!

Dad, Daddy, Pop, Papa, Papi:
If you are able, give her a ride on your back,
and you will forever gallop in her heart.

NOBODY KNOWS

Nobody knows secrets hidden so deep
Nobody knows the pain I keep.

Nobody knows of secrets forever buried, secrets whose bones
have now dissolved into the earth, but whose ghosts lurk still.

Nobody knows the feel of the nightmarish crawl
of an unauthorized touch.

Nobody knows of the perplexity of a child
whose innocence was viciously confiscated.

Nobody knows of the ceaseless anxiety of a child
witnessing their pendulum of sanity slowly shear away.

Nobody knows of the paralyzing fear of a child, whose tiny sliver of
confidence was drained by an unredeemed, menacing brute.

Nobody knows the sting of torrential merciless insults
which sprung from kith and kin.

Nobody knows the horrendous dejection
of being entrapped in a cave of vocal impediment and rebuked for it and
abandoned by an unextended hand.

Nobody knows the humiliation of puking during school recess
and have your innards betray you
and mock your socioeconomic status.

Nobody knows of the searing pain of having to conceal
the holes in one's heart and the discomfiture
of having to conceal the holes in one's tennis shoes.

Nobody knows how it feels to have an adolescence preempted and a
womanhood thwarted by the forbidden sights
of a child's casting eyes.

Nobody knows of the insatiable hunger
for paternal love and validation.

Nobody knows the disappointment of inheriting a legacy
of what *not* to be.

Nobody knows the singe of racing fiery terrors
heaped on a child's heart and mind—terrors that would punctuate every
chapter of that child's life.

Nobody knows how it feels to have a destiny intercepted
because no one could see the dread in a child's eyes
and offer some reassurance.

Nobody knows the torment of haunting cries
forever echoing from a foreboding past.

Nobody knows of the incredulity of having vicious, venomous propaganda
plastered on one's emotional billboards.

Nobody knows of the unspeakable corporal thrashing
committed by a despicable, sinister, loathsome, and cowardly beast.

Nobody knows the wrath and the unyielding crush of being trampled
underfoot by a posturing, tarnished, dethroned charlatan.

Nobody knows of the immense, stoical resolution required to gird oneself
as an unflinching target
for the startling rupture of a cool, smooth ominous bullet.

Nobody knows of the warped sensation of summoning death
and entreating its arrival as a breezy, welcoming relief.

The abominations of the past remain interred;
never to be voluntarily exhumed and unveiled, for the anguish of it all
would be too great a burden for any other to bear.

Nobody knows secrets hidden so deep

Nobody knows the pain I keep
Nobody.

SCARED NO MORE

("May you have sweet rest, Nicole.")

I forced myself to look
Looked right down there into that cold, dark pit
Looked right down into that unrelenting, unforgiving grotto of death
Looked at death's snarling tentacles
Anxiously waiting to embrace a lifeless casing
Looked right down at its gloating, impatient smirk glaring up at me
That vulturous, imperialistic pit of darkness
Claiming a hollow victory over a lovely, adorned shell.

Then, something forced me to look up
Slowly, I looked all around and realized I was scared no more
     My fears disappeared as her soft pink casket
        was gently lowered into the wood-walled cavern.
     My fears disappeared as thrown fuchsia
        petals cast wilted kisses onto the sun-tanned coffin.
     My fears disappeared as hurled untilled soil
        reluctantly swirled in a descending dance.
     My fears disappeared as ruddy water streamed
        into the cavern, fluffing the turf for eternity's rest.
     My fears disappeared as a cultivated carpet of luminous
        emerald sod was hastily placed on the subtle mound.
     My fears disappeared as the ground's neighboring seedlings
        linked in a seamless mesh.

Unexpectedly, there was a sound, a soft ruffling of flapping wings.
Peering out from a woven basket, twenty-one reticent, velvety white
doves materialized and, straight away, took flight. Stunned, I watched
in amazement as my departing fears leapt up, bound themselves to
the wings of the doves, and hitched a ride.

In disbelief, I blinked and opened my eyes wide; just in time to behold
my fears dissipate into oblivion with each flutter of the doves' wings. The
doves hovered in a brief farewell, then soared to their great known.
I straightened up, and I realized I was scared no more
She was at rest, and I was scared no more. Scared no more of death!

THE 4 *M*'S

(My Mama, My Money, My Meat, and My Man)

There are four things very important to me
I'll try to explain them if I can
And remember not to ever mess with them
They're my mama, my money, my meat, and my man.

Don't mess with my mama, whatever you do
Because she's quite important to me
And if the slightest harm ever comes to her
You will suffer a great penalty.

And please don't fool with any of my money
For I work too hard to get it
And if I find that even one dime is missing
You most surely will regret it.

And don't touch my meat when it's on my plate
Oh no! Please! Don't dare!
For if you ask me for what you want
I will be most willing to share.

Well, that brings me down to my man
And I'll tell you what I'll do
Whenever I am through with him
I'll send him on to you.

So now, you have been duly forewarned
And I've explained it the best I can
And I advise you not to ever mess with
My mama, my money, my meat, and my man.

I HEARD WHAT YOU *DIDN'T* SAY

I heard what you said
Although you didn't utter a sound
But your meaning came through clearly
Through your insidious frown.

I heard what you said
Although your lips moved not
As your reluctant expression
Revealed your loathsome thought.

I heard what you said
Although from your mouth came not a word
Oh! If only my ears could see
What my eyes have heard.

I heard what you said
And I know what you meant
Although your lips weren't moving
Your face exposed a hint.

So be careful what you say
When from your lips, no words may fall
For while my ears may hear nothing
My eyes hear all.

MY OLD IRON

I had an old iron
It was very old, and it was very heavy
I bought it at a flea market
I immediately noticed that the cord was awfully frayed
Duct tape had salvaged the cord many times
But the old iron still looked as if it had some use.

It turned out that the iron only worked at its convenience
It didn't heat evenly
And it was always threatening to burn my clothes
You had to watch that iron real close
Because it might catch on fire any minute
But I really liked that iron.

Now, I could afford a new iron
But I found some contentment with that old iron
By and by, that old iron became dangerous
The raggedy cord actually sparked a couple of times
I'd unplug the iron, and I'd blow out the sparks
But I kept right on using it.

One morn, I was ironing my favorite dress (the red silk one)
And that old iron caught on fire
There were flames everywhere
Well, that was it
That darn iron had to go
Its time was up.

After all that, I still had to convince myself to throw that iron away
Finally, I got a pair of scissors, and I cut the cord off completely
I threw the iron and the cord away
Now, there would be no going back
I bought a brand-new iron
It works just fine.

***Sometimes you may have to cut the cord
because not everything can be taped up.***

BROKE

I gambled my happiness on layaway love
Pawned my emotional sanity for the sake of a fool
Gave my heart to an emotionally bankrupt twerp
Bargained my soul at the devil's yard sale
Bartered my salvation in exchange for the temporal
Surrendered everything I had to an undeserving parasite
And now, I'm broke

Actually, I *was* broke
But then, something happened, and I awoke
I was ready to stop being broke and break free
And be broke no more

So I went back to the source of my being
Took out a mortgage on my salvation
Got a lifetime guarantee on a fully renewable loan
No threat of recall, reversal, or foreclosure
Yes! I went back
Newly redeemed, I reclaimed all my stuff
Reclaimed my happiness and my emotional sanity
Reclaimed my heart, my soul, and my salvation

I *was* broke
Broke and bound
Bewildered and beguiled
Baffled and bamboozled

But now, I'm broke no more
I'm bound no more
Now, I'm free
And because I'm free, I'm rich indeed!

WHY?

You stretched a ladder to the moon
        and plucked a star from its midst for me

You methodically reconfigured the elements of the firmament
        for my earthly bliss

You procured the infinite and superfluous gains of the universe,
        and you nestled them at my feet

You unbarred, unlatched, and unchained
        your vaulted, imprisoned heart so I could enter

You renounced all that was dear to you
        so that you might forever prove your eternal love for me

And for all my other desires, you summoned and commissioned
        a phalanx of angels and mortals to serve me

If you could do all those things for me
Then, please tell me . . . please tell me . . .
Why was my simple request that you bring nothing less than honesty to my
door a virtual impossibility for you to accomplish?

Why?

Why?

Why?

LAYAWAY LOVE

Some men browse through women the way they browse through a rack of clothes. They pick up a woman here, pick up a woman there, toss stuff in the cart, and stroll around with it for a while.

They can't decide what they want; they've got to look at *everything*.
Look! *That* one looks good!
I think I'll try it on to see how it fits.
Oh! I really like the color and style of *that* one over there too.
Yeah! *That's* the one I want—*that* one right there!
Ooooh! Look at *that* one. *That's* what I'm talkin' about!
I know it doesn't go with anything I have, but I've got to have it.
But wait a minute, look at *that* one in the display window.
I know I've already got one like it at home, but I want *that* too.
Yeah! *That's* the one I really, really want—I think.

At the checkout, they discover they have insufficient means.
But since they've got to have *that* and *that* and *that* too, they put everything on layaway. They put down a little measly deposit to hold the layaway, and every now and then, they come back to check on it. They put in a little time, put down a few dimes.

Now, there are a few problems with layaways:
Sometimes folks *forget* to go back and retrieve layaways.

Sometimes layaways just languish in storage, and if they are finally claimed, they may be *out of season* and really won't get much wear.

Sometimes unclaimed layaways are put back in circulation, but by then, they may be *out of style*, and of course, their demand is usually low.

Sometimes folks even *lose* their layaway claim ticket, but since they didn't put that much down on it anyway, it's no big loss.

So, brothers:
When you're out shopping or out "just looking,"
if your accessibility can't meet your desirability,
LEAVE IT ON THE RACK!

IT'S OVER NOW

I gave all to you
And with you, I was fair
I trusted all with you
And now, my heart's in despair.

You just took from me
And you gave nothing in return
Then, you walked away
And you showed no concern
For my broken heart
Or my shattered mind
And my wondrous love
Will I ever find?

But it's over now
And I wonder how
I ever fell for you.

NEED IS A FOUR-LETTER WORD

Occasionally, I've been asked why I'm not married, and I usually give my usual answer:

> *"I haven't found the man who deserves me yet."*

I said that to one of my church sisters, Sister Ledbetter, and do you know what she said to me?

> She said, "Sugar, that's all right, you don't need a man;
> all you need is Jesus."

Well, you can't imagine what I said to her.

> I told her, "Dear sister, that's easy for you to say when you've got Deacon Ledbetter lolling up next to you every night, snoring in your face." Humph!

Now, one thing about it, Sister Ledbetter was right.

> I don't *need* a man.

You see, I've observed that *need* occasionally keeps company with *dependency*, and where you find *dependency*, you will probably find their first cousin, *control*. Now, let's be clear—this is not a reference to normal, fundamental *need*, because some relational need is requisite. This reference is to the type of *need* where your identity, your self-regard, and your self-worth are so intrinsically wired into the circuitry of another being to the extent that your very existence may be dependent upon your link to this being.

Sisters, when you *need* a man and he knows that you *need* him, you are ripe for manipulation. He can do anything to you (if you allow it) and will do anything to you (if you allow it), and you're helpless (or so you think), and you will take all of his mess because you *need* him. Sometimes, your *need* is simply a benign dependence; sometimes it's a severe, malignant codependence.

So what's a girl to do?

> Don't *need* him
> Don't allow yourself to *need* him if it's to your own detriment
> Love him! Want him! Desire him! Adore him!
> But don't *need* him!
> Girls, the minute you *need* him, you are in TROUBLE!

YOU DON'T DESERVE MY LOVE

I've tried
Oh! How I've tried
To be with you
And stay by your side
But it's hard to do
When I can't trust you
To be honest with our love
But I'm moving on
And with you, I'm done
Because you don't deserve my love.

I've given
I've given all that I can
Because no one else
Would lend you a hand
But you didn't appreciate
Until it was much too late
And you weren't honest with our love
But I'm moving on
And with you, I'm done
Because you don't deserve my love.

You abused me, and you misused me
While we were dating, you were waiting
For the moment to bring me down
But I'm moving on
And with you, I'm done
Because you don't deserve my love
And don't think that "I'm sorry" is going to change everything
You've been sorry so many times before
But before you have the chance to hurt me again
I'm walking right out the door.

Yes! I'm moving on
And with you, I'm done
Because you don't deserve my love.

HAPPILY SINGLE

I
would
rather
have
nothing
instead
of
taking
anything
just
so
I
can
say
I've
got
something

LADIES, LISTEN UP!

(We Take Too Long to Get Tired)

Why do you let him bring foolishness to your door
And why do you tolerate his devious lies?
You don't have time to be bothered with fools
And for his games, you're much too wise.

You should take the time to closely examine
The things he promises to do
And if they don't enhance, encourage, or uplift
Then, tell me, what can he do for you?

The possibilities are great that others possess
All that you've been searching for
And you can potentially get what you *think* you've got
And perhaps, even more.

Because your life didn't begin with that one man
And with him, it surely won't end
So there's no need for you to act as if
Your total existence, upon him, depends.

Because if he can't contribute to your happiness
Then there's little purpose in your life he can meet
Don't let him subdue your spirit
And your energy, don't let him deplete.

But always remember the essence of your being
In your resolve, be most unswerving
And because you deserve the best in life
Never offer yourself to the undeserving.

SEPARATING THE MEN FROM THE BOYS

All men to the front
All boys to the rear
I have a few words
I'd like you to hear.

Some of you are masquerading
As men, though boys you be
And it causes great confusion
When the differences you don't see.

You see, many differences exist between a boy and a man
Some of them, you obviously forgot
And so for your edification
Let's just examine what being a man is *not*.

It's not what's in your pockets
It's not what's in your pants
It's not your seductive smile
Or your bold and cocky stance.

It's not the fancy clothes you wear
Or that nauseating cologne
It's not your jingle-jangle
Or that car that you don't own.

It's not your weak one-liners
That you lay on the sisters in the street
Because a boy can only lay down a promise
But a man won't make a promise that he can't keep.

No! Being a man is about the realization
That you have been especially called
And you must answer whenever your trumpet sounds
And give it your very all.

So to those of you yet standing in the rear
Will you step up to the plate and take a stand?
Because it's late in the evening, and it's time, my brothers
To separate the boy from the man.

All men to the front
All boys to the rear
And the rest of you clowns can get up
And get outta here!

MEN

Ladies?

You are expecting an extracted, overwrought expose calculated to emasculate men, aren't you? Well, you may be disappointed.

What can be said about men that hasn't already been defrosted, sliced, diced, warmed, and served up as a hot appetizer?

There's no need to dissect every component of a man
just to relegate him to an abyss of nonvirility.

And there's no need to elaborate on the all-consuming mythological sexual prowess of men when it's already known that a good measure of that is overrated and under delivered a good deal of the time.

Men are
> human and inhuman, as are we
> honorable and dishonorable, as are we
> erudite and ignorant, as are we
> compassionate and emotionally constipated, as are we
> defensive and offensive, as are we
> and they are benevolent and malevolent, as are we.

Men can be all of those things, none of those things,
and all in between. Men can be everything to us, nothing to us,
and all in between.

There are boys
There are males
There are men; then, there are all the others

But whatever you think men are
Whatever you think men aren't
Whatever you think men ought to be
And however men treat you and respond to you
Consider that *some* of the onus may rest on *your* shoulders.

Men: They Simply Are.

SUITE 4

ENCOURAGEMENT AND INSPIRATION

PERFECT PEACE

There's a perfect peace deep in my heart
It permeates the very core of me
It encourages me to smile, even through tears
It comes from the Lord, you see.

It saturates all that surrounds me
Even the simplest things
It causes my eyes to marvel at life
And it compels my heart to sing.

It's the flow that entreats me to love
Even my fiercest foe
It's the force that allows me to forgive
Even the harshest blow.

This abundance of peace is a wondrous blessing
Bestowed especially upon me
And without its daily renewal
I don't dare to think where I'd be.

But you too can have this perfect peace
The Lord can plant it in your heart
You only need to seek His face
And His love, He will impart.

You must go to Him with sincerity
Implore Him to calm your soul
But be resolved to follow His course
And stay within the fold.

His peace will comfort you in times of trouble
It will blanket you in the midst of despair
And your portion will never be depleted
For He continually replenishes your share.

Now, while all else may not be perfect in your life
At least your heart will find its content
And you will have life more abundantly
Because that is why He was sent.

And if you keep your eyes stayed on Him
Submit yourself, and let unrighteousness cease
And then, you will know no greater joy
As when He grants you perfect peace.

HE UNDERSTANDS

If your heart is hurting
And your spirit is torn
And you feel all hope is gone
Don't be discouraged
Don't be dismayed
For you are not alone.

There is one who'll hear you
There is one who cares
There is one who'll hold your hand
For just when you think
All else has failed
Remember, Jesus understands
Remember, Jesus understands!

HE COMFORTS

If you are suffering with pain and sorrow
And for your loved one, your heart does grieve
I come to tell you that comfort waits for those
Who in Him, do believe.

Yes! He hears your groaning, and He sees your tears
And your pain, He must surely feel
But there is no sorrow upon this earth
That our Heavenly Father cannot heal.

So lean upon Him in your time of need
Entreat Him in secret prayer
For I know that He will surely hear your call
And your burdens, He will bear.

LOOK TO THE CROSS

The
Lord
sends
His
blessings
but asks
little
of us
to give.
He only wants for us to look to Him and live.
Look ever unto the Lord; on Him, lean and depend,
for
man
may
often
fail
you,
but
He's
always
your
friend.

FROM MORNING TILL NIGHT

Rise in the morning
To greet the dawn of day
Bask in the beauty
Of its golden sunshine rays.

And then, move through the hours
Let each moment live in your heart
Because once an instant has passed
Of it, you'll never again be a part.

And finally, lie down in the night light
Give thanks for all that has been
And pray that tomorrow's blessings
Upon you again, He will send.

HE IS OUR HOPE

We live in a world that is often
Ugly, cold, and mean
We are surrounded by many dangers
Some discernable; others hideously unseen.

And the pressures of daily life
Can sometimes seem too much to bear
Yet we must remember to hold on
We surely must not despair.

For truly there is hope for us
That will ease our pain and sorrow
For though we may suffer today
We must believe there's a brighter tomorrow.

Our hope lies in our Heavenly Father
Who keeps watch over us from above
And showers down upon us
His precious and bountiful love.

Yes! He alone can keep us
For He came that we might have life
And He surely must be saddened
To see us wrestle with pain and strife.

But if we lean wholly upon Him
He will give us life abundantly
And hope will live in us forever
And with Him, we will dwell eternally.

YOU BETTER COME CLEAN WITH GOD

Sure, nobody saw you when you stole that money
And besides, you needed it real bad
      But if you don't repent and come clean with God
      My friend, you're going to wish you had.

Oh! And only a few folks heard you when you told that lie
It's okay. Maybe no harm will be done
      But you better repent because lies come back to visit
      And the Lord, you can never outrun.

And you did nothing wrong when you slandered your sister
After all, you were just telling the truth
      But you better repent and come clean with God
      Remember, He knows a whole lot more about you.

And that gossip that you've been carrying all over town
Why, you were just trying to keep folks informed
      But you better repent and come clean with God
      For one day, He'll have to weather your storm.

And there's no problem with your having a little fun
Why, it's only a little harmless dope
      But you better repent and come clean with God
      For He is your only hope.

      You need to change your attitude and your actions
      You need to begin the transformation without delay
      Because for all your evildoing, you may get by
      But you will never completely get away.

      The Father knows and sees all you do and say
      He knows every path you've trod
      I tell you, my friend, you better repent
      And you better come clean with God.

WHERE YOU GONNA SIT WHEN YOU GIT TO HEBBEN?

Tell me where you gonna sit when you git to hebben
Tell me where you gonna sit when you meet with the Lawd
If we don't git along down here, we won't git along up there
Tell me where you gonna sit when you git to hebben.

Why do I ask?
    A long time ago, *some* white folk had a problem
    They made us sit at the back of the bus
    And that really got me to wonderin'
    If we all make it to hebben, will they sit with the rest of us?

So tell me where you gonna sit when you git to hebben
Tell me where you gonna sit when you meet with the Lawd
If we don't git along down here, we won't even make it up there
Tell me where you gonna sit when you git to hebben.

Well, I don't care where I sit just as long as I git to hebben
I don't care where I sit when I meet with the Lawd
If the vict'ry, I do win
I'll sho' 'nuff make it in
And I don't care where I sit when I git to hebben.

But I'll tell you where I'm gonna sit when I git to hebben
I'll tell you where I'm gonna sit when I meet with the Lawd
If I follow where God leads
Humph! I'll sit where I darn well please
That's where I'm gonna sit when I git to hebben.

When I git to hebben
When I git to hebben
I'm gonna sit with my Lawd
Hallelujah! Hallelujah!
I'm gonna sit with my Lawd!

A PRAYER

Dear Lord, we humbly bow
Before your throne of grace
Asking for your blessings
Upon this human race.

We need you, Lord, this very minute
In our hearts and in our heads
For we live in a world that's too often
Filled with hate and dread.

We pray that you stay close by us
We pray that you never leave our side
And we pray that you will forever
In our hearts, abide.

MAMEE

(A Dedication of Love, from Your Children)

It is easy to write these words of dedication
Because you are so easy to love
And every day, we give thanks for you
To our Heavenly Father above.

We thank Him for giving you to us
Because in His infinite wisdom, He knew
The trials that we would encounter in life
And He knew no other mother would do.

You not only gave us your very best
You gave us your very all
And only you were there to pick us up
From our many slips and falls.

Mamee, we know we can never thank you enough
On that, we unanimously agree
And without your love, devotion, and guidance
We dare not think where we'd be.

So all we can say is that we love you
Although we've said it a thousand times
And when God was issuing out mothers
I'm so glad He made you mine!

THE FAMILY

Once upon a time, born to a lady so sweet
    Were eleven superb children that I'd like you to meet.
One is a preacher and one is a teacher
    One is a quiet, mysterious creature.
One has a reputation for being mean
    One of them was awfully hard to wean.
One, they used to say, would always go and tattle
    One of them is rather hard to rattle.
One, they say, always acts like the boss
    One has a mean streak you don't want to cross.
One enjoys living his life from the shores
    One is the person everybody adores.
One doesn't hesitate to speak his mind
    One will tell you in a minute to kiss his behind.
One used to be mean, but now is quite mellow
    He's become a Sunday-morning-church-going fellow.
One is very private and works very hard
    One thinks of himself with such high regard.
One was rebellious and lived life with no remorse
    Happily, he's reformed and is on a brand-new course.
All the boys have married, and all of them are fathers
    Except for one, I guess, who figured, "Why bother?"
Their wives are fine ladies, and all are first-rate
    They're perfectly suited, devoted mates.
The girls are quite stunning and are hard to forget
    They haven't found the one who deserves them yet.
Nieces and nephews and cousins untold
    Oh! Such great potential, their futures hold.
And though we don't always see eye to eye
    There's much love in the family, and this, no one can deny.
And though the family may sometimes wear thin
    I wouldn't trade the world for my family and kin.
We wonderfully descended from our dear, sweet Mamee
    Which proves that the apples don't fall far from the tree.

***Love your kinfolk whether you like them or not;
you can't choose your family, but they're all that you've got.***

THE GIFT OF GIVING

(Lessons Learned at Mamee's Knee)

I learned the gift of giving
From my mother a long time ago
When she impressed these words upon me:
"You will reap just what you sow."

She taught us to give by example
To the strangers who came to our door
For she would often give them our very last
And we wouldn't have any more.

And we children would be so astonished
Because her words, we didn't understand:
"Children, I don't know if they can do without this,
But I do know that I can."

And her spirit of giving lives in me
In my heart, it is deeply imbedded
And though some may take my giving for granted
The giving, I've never regretted.

And I love you, dear mother, for teaching me to give
For I think it's the best part of me
And I've tried to live by your example
So that Christ, in me, others will see.

I advise you to take my mother's teachings
And for others, do the best you can do
Because the good that you do for others
Will most surely come back to you.

MISS MAGNOLIA

It's almost seven-fifteen
Miss Magnolia will be walking by pretty soon
We wait for her to walk by every morning
There she is, in her crisply starched white uniform
We watch her sail by—she's moving pretty fast this morning
Look at her flaming red hair just flowing in the wind
Look at her glide across that pavement
Look! Miss Magnolia actually swishes when she walks.

She's on her way to work at Mrs. Noel's big antebellum house
There will be lots of chores waiting for her there
Baskets of bloomers, brassieres, and girdles need to be soaked
Cottony soft cashmere sweaters need to be aired on the clothesline
Culottes and pedal pushers need to be washed, starched, and ironed
Fine table linens and fine bed linens need to be changed
Hardwood floors need to be scrubbed and waxed
Flowered wallpaper needs to be gingerly wiped down
Manor furniture need be polished and buffed
Heirloom crystal and silverware need to be glistened
A whole slab of prime beef needs to be tenderized and roasted
After supper is served, dishes need to be washed, dried, and put up.

It's almost seven-fifteen
Miss Magnolia will be walking back by pretty soon
We wait for her to walk by every evening
Her white uniform is stale, wrinkled, and slightly stained now
We watch her slowly drift by on her way home
Her red hair is flat with sweat, but it's still flaming
Her body is aching, and her feet ignore her silent commands
Her walk is a lot softer now, and her swish is gone.

Miss Magnolia toiled almost twelve hours today
Her mind is churned up from the white lady's unrelenting "requests"
Miss Magnolia didn't earn but a few dollars today
Just enough to pay the burial insurance man
But it's honest money—thank the Lord
She's also got a pocketful of dignity earned through hard work.
Dignity (not disdain) can be gained from hard, earnest work.

MUCH HARVESTING

Last night was restless
The morn brings welcome relief
And soon, I must rise
For much harvesting awaits
Harvesting must not be late.

Yesterday was cruel
Its yoke was unrelenting
It was so callous
My every step was mocked
My systems are now in shock.

I need to slow down
I want the world to slow down
So I can get off
I'll find a big shady tree
Sit in its bough silently.

I'll be still and quiet
I'll listen to the silence
World, come back later
I will once again feel whole
Sanity rejoins my soul.

The night dim has gone
The morn brings welcome relief
And now, I must rise
For much harvesting awaits
Harvesting must not be late.

RHYTHMS OF LIFE

flirting leaves on waltzing trees
      clanging urban cacophonies
trains, planes, and motorcars
      inane mockery in smutty bars
bikes, carts, and shuffling feet
      grazing on patched and ragged streets
shadows long on roast-hot days
      offspring frolicking in summer's haze
rain pellets unrelentingly smack
      overgrown roots in cement cracks
birds in flight, circling high
      ground-bound creatures fume and sigh
infant's wails, quickly assuaged
      mother's nerves, badly frayed
young lass laughing, coyly feign
      innocence shortly to remain
young lad arrogant, boldly crude
      defiant, provocative attitude
vulgar eruptions, vicious, profane
      ambiguous expulsions from the mentally insane
hustlers, players, and wannabes
      dispensing recycled misery
broken hearts, wailing in rhyme
      neighborhoods seized by senseless crime
prophetic voices on corners proclaim
      judicial gavels dispensing blame
stale romance, together yet apart
      silent contempt in hardened hearts
sleepy yawns cast aside
      night's libidos lurking wide
a chanteuse's haunting serenade
      beastly horrors on beds displayed
speaking eyes where no one peers
      silence loud, but no one hears
happy celebrations, spirits chime
      a mortal's final breath, out of time

Listen, and you may truly hear the tantalizing rhythms of life.

MUSIC

Music
Beautiful, Dolce
Inspiring, Singing, Comforting
Joyful, Sacred, Spiritual, Vital
Refreshing, Anointing, Encompassing
Blissful, Sensuous
Me

FREE

I've lived my life in bondage
I've lived my life in chains
I've lived my life entangled
Lived a life of pain

I've lived a life of wand'ring
I've lived a life of doubt
I've lived a life not knowing
What my life's about

But now it's time to break the chains from my mind
It's time to break the chains from my heart
It's time to break the chains from my soul
And finally be free
God did not intend that we live our lives in chains
From sin and disobedience, look what remains
Yet He reaches out His hand to you and me
If we accept it, we can be free

He can free us from the darkness, the hurt, and the agony
He can give us blessed assurance, and with Him, we can be free
He can help us to release the demons from our wicked past
He'll make us free at last
He can free us to look forward and not at what's behind
He can free us to receive the blessings that are yours and mine
He can free us to forgive abuse that's hurled at you and me
He'll help us to be free
He can free us from the fear and guilt of dreams yet unfulfilled
He can free us to the courage to accept His holy will
He can free us from depression, gloom, and misery
He wants us to be free

Misuse, abuse, excuse
Release them
They have no use.

May you be restored, and may you be free.

HAPPINESS

Happiness
Ecstatic, Explosive
Singing, Loving, Laughing
Caviar, Champagne, Catfish, Collard Greens
Playing, Dancing, Kissing
Blessed, Serene
Family

CELEBRATE LIFE!

Celebrate your birthdays with gladness
Celebrate them all with glee
Don't be like some folk who are ashamed of their age
Be thankful for each birthday you see.

Yes! Count up all your glorious years
Remember them one by one
Relish the positive experiences you've had
And don't worry about what you could have done.

Enjoy each day that you are given
Live life fully in all that you do
And don't waste time worrying about tomorrow
Remember, it isn't promised to you.

DO YOU KNOW WHERE YOU'RE GOING?

Do you know the purpose
For which you were created
And what you're doing with your life
Is it at all related?

And have you taken the time
To question your reason for being
Or perhaps you already know it
But from it, you are fleeing?

You see, each of us in life
Is called to a special task
But regardless of what we choose to do
Only what we do for Christ will last.

So don't live your life without discovering
What it is He wants you to do
And make sure that you're on the path
That He has chosen for you.

DON'T GIVE IN!
DON'T GIVE OUT!
DON'T GIVE UP!

The paths of life are full of joys
Boundless, beyond imagination
But they also harbor turmoil and great troubles
That may challenge one's determination.

And when your goals in life are threatened
And disappointment you begin to feel
Don't be dismayed, and don't be discouraged
And to failure, you mustn't yield.

But delve deep down into your spirit's well
Where you'll find strength and reserves of fortitude
And then, spring forth with a new endowment
And a newly resolved attitude.

And don't worry about matters that are in the past
"If only" is only fruitless words
But press on forward toward your goals
And with confidence, may your spirit be gird.

Believe in yourself and in your capabilities
And don't host undermining doubt
To your fears, don't give in; on your goals, don't give up
But keep on striving, and never ever give out.

DESTINY

Dream from your heart, and let your spirit see
The place in the universe where you are meant to be.

Then get there.

JUST KEEP ON!

Don't worry about the harvest
    Just keep on tilling your soil
Don't worry about how you will make a way
    The Father, The Way Maker, has already made the way
    All you have to do is move into His way!

Don't worry about yesterday
    Yesterday is gone
Don't worry about tomorrow
    Tomorrow is not yours yet
    Relish today, for all you have is **now**!

Don't worry about what anybody else has
    Don't worry about what anybody else is doing
Just keep on doing what *you* have been called to do
    While in this place, just do your part
    Just keep on! Just keep on! Just keep on!

THE TRIUMPH OF LIGHT

The atrocities in our lives can assuredly be asphyxiated
by spiritual exertion, and even then,
their tentacles will yet strain to breathe.

But they can *never* eclipse the luminosity
that emanates from your soul!

DON'T WORRY 'BOUT THE MULE;
YOU JUST LOAD THE WAGON.

That's all.

Cover Concept And Design
Flash & Flair

Cover Photographs:
F. Wilkins

TO OBTAIN ADDITIONAL COPIES OF
Not for Rent, Sale, or Lease

Email:
www.notforrentsaleorlease@yahoo.com

OR

Write:
Velma DuPont
P.O. Box 230954
Boston, MA 02123

Printed in the United States
200867BV00005B/100-111/A